Are extenuating circumstances weighing you down?

Here are 15 steps to empower your life

Sometimes you may have situations that weigh you down, impact your beliefs, and affect your approach and outlook on life. Perhaps it's the challenges of racism, discrimination, harassment, and even overcoming a personal battle with your health.

With enthusiasm about sharing the tools to enhance your forward momentum towards your empowerment Natalie Clayton has written this Itty Bitty® book to give you the systems to see your inner strength and claim your light.

In this book you will learn:

- To be resilient
- To welcome change
- To keep calm in the storm
- To be a vessel for victory
- And so much more!

If you are ready to make empowering changes in your life and let your light shine through, then pick up a copy of this transformative Itty Bitty® Book Today!

Your Amazing
Itty Bitty®

Awaken the
Leader Within

15 Steps To Shine Your Light

Natalie J. Clayton, MS

Published by Itty Bitty® Publishing
A subsidiary of S & P Productions, Inc.

Copyright © 2021 **Natalie J. Clayton, MS**

Printed in the United States of America

Itty Bitty Publishing
311 Main Street, Suite D
El Segundo, CA 90245
(310) 640-8885

ISBN: 978-1-950326-92-1

Dedication Page

This book is dedicated to my three amazing children, Natasha, Namar, Nigel, and my three adorable grandchildren, Nylah, Nasir, and Anoki.

In addition, to my late amazing beloved parents, George T. and Irene E. Clayton, Sr.

Stop by our Itty Bitty® website to find interesting blog entries regarding personal development and leadership.

www.IttyBittyPublishing.com

Or visit Natalie J. Clayton at

www.tiltsynergyinc.com

www.nataliejclatyon.com

Table of Contents

Awaken the Leader Within
15 Steps To Shine Your Light

Did you know that you have a leader within? Sometimes extenuating situations can weigh you down, impact your beliefs, and affect your approach and outlook on life.

For over two decades, I dedicated myself to a career as a professional law enforcement officer in Southern California. I worked in diverse communities to protect, serve and impact the lives of others.

As a believer in God, along with faith, tenacity and thought leadership, these helped me get through challenges of racism, discrimination, harassment, and overcome a personal battle with stage 3 cancer.

This book is written to give you the tools to see your light. I am enthusiastic about sharing these tools to enhance your forward movement toward your light.

Be bold, authentic, assertive, confident, and resilient through transitions and transformations, for change will come.

Let there be light.

~ Natalie J. Clayton

Step 1
Resilience

Resilience is the process of being agile well into the face of adversity, challenges, and significant crisis. For example, in law enforcement undercover work is an analytical and militant mindset for adaptation in uncertain and unchartered waters. Resilience allows you to:

1. Get into shape
2. Recover readily
3. Become strong

When you experience challenges and chaotic situations in life, whether in the capacity of your professional career or personal life, the best way to get through and overcome them starts with the belief that you can do it. You will then achieve the power of resilience.

Even if you can't see it with the naked eye, belief is a strong force of positive energy that happens in your mind. So, make your positive energy the main thing. The belief system you have inside is the result of your world on the outside. Resilience dwells in belief, but it is created in your spirit.

Elements of Resilience

How do you see yourself? Are you a victim, survivor, navigator, or thriver?

- **Are you in shape?** Getting back in the game is preparing yourself mentally and emotionally. When you do this, your body will follow. Everything you think/ believe about yourself or your situation determines the outcome of everything else that happens to you.
- **How do you recover?** Proactive faith in belief and active pursuit of balanced wellness leads to success in recovery.
- **Are you becoming strong?** Acquiring strength requires action, owning responsibility, adopting an attitude of will power, a ferrous warrior mentality, and establishing inner authority.

The benefit of mindfulness can build resilience and increase positive emotions, which reduce negative energy, emotion, and stress.

Mindfulness:

- Fosters trust
- Adopts a growth mindset
- Focuses on your strengths

Step 2
Catalyst for Change

Change is a certainty in life. Its purpose is to make better or transform. Effecting change in your life requires a decision and the ability to change, which occurs with different responses in various situations. Change can be viewed as difficult, but is possible when you believe.

According to C.S Lewis, "You can't go back and change the beginning, but you can start where you are and change the ending."

How do you become a catalyst for change? Have you ever seen or experienced something that is unjust towards others? Did the situation leave a negative impact that still needs to be addressed? Think about this: are there people waiting and depending on you to effect change?

Be the change.

Elements of change:

1. People (cultural and social norms)
2. Emotions
3. Mental health
4. Belief systems
5. Organizational (structure and leadership)

Transformational Change

You may desire to reorient your thinking and beliefs to change things in your life. However, sometimes fear takes over, and distracts you from getting to see the tools available for you to work with. This obstacle can cause a misfire in your jumpstart to transformation.

- **To make better or transform:** Transformation is an act of processes through which something becomes different and better.
- **Catalyst for change:** A catalyst can be an inner conviction of personal growth or self-awareness and authenticity. To be accountable, to take initiative. It's often a collaborative effort with the capacity for others to model and follow.

Change is something that affects everyone. Yet people find initiating or sustaining change to be very difficult. However, it is not impossible.

"Intelligence is the ability to adapt to change."
- Stephen Hawking

Step 3
Universalize Something New

Behold, I will do something new, now it will spring forth: Will you not be aware of it? (Isaiah 43:19)

You can do something radically different and new! You may be facing a major decision in life or a fork in the road. Do you have a dream or a vision that may change the world as we see it? Do you get excited about creating a plan, or do you push it aside and make excuses?

New concepts require:

1. Vision
2. Transparency
3. Values

Creating something new can be as simple as allowing the "new" to enter and staying open to opportunities. Do you sense the excitement of doing something new?

For example, your desire to start a new business, the purchase of a new car, or better yet, a new house.

Every day you wake up there is an opportunity to do something new. Get your thoughts and visions in order. Don't let worry, or internal obstacles stop you from doing what has been put in your heart to do.

Universalize Vision, Transparency, Values

A crisis often creates ambiguity and continuous evaluations for the best available path moving forward. Clarity is a necessity that includes developing a future vision with optimism, research, knowledge, and intentions toward success.

- **Vision:** Create a compelling vision both short and long-term that leads to future success. This provides you and your team with hope, and grounds people in the knowledge that things will get better.
- **Transparency:** Have ongoing conversations and processes that are visible and understood by everyone responsible for the outcome. The transparency must be defined by a common standard and a shared understanding of what works and what doesn't work.
- **Values:** Your commitment, positive attitude, and core values serve as guardrails in making key decisions to enable people in your organization to thrive.

According to the great Albert Einstein, "The significant problems we face cannot be solved at the same level of thinking we were at when we created them."

Step 4
Stay Connected

Your ability to connect and interact is priceless.
Patience leads to opening the door to understand
an individual's stance.

"Nobody is superior, nobody is inferior, but
nobody is equal either. People are simply unique
and incomparable."   *- Osho*

Connection requires:

1. Communication strategy
2. Engagement
3. Alignment

Connecting with people is the nucleus to building
solid relationships. It can create and bring support
in the physical and mental wellbeing of another
human being.

Social connections can help lower anxiety, reduce
depression, lead to higher self-esteem and
empathy. In the current state and present day,
relationship engagement is powerful.

There is no "I" in a team. Team collaboration is
important. Teamwork can create and foster faster
results and foster dreamwork.

Connect, Communicate, Engage, Align

When you connect and engage with an individual or in a team setting and you all speak the same language, the result is commitment, cause and change initiatives. This can create an avenue for timely and accurate information that can positively influence awareness with the acceptance of feelings and thoughts. This simple act can remove resistance to change.

- **Communication strategy:** Choose effective routines that carry collaborative efforts designed to achieve support that keeps team members informed. This strategy enables team members to receive information and deliver feedback to build a trusting relationship.
- **Engagement:** The process by which individuals of an organization or company aspire to be better. Getting better requires a clear understanding of what they want, what they need, when they need it, and how they expect to receive it.
- **Alignment:** Maintain alignment on practical matters such as processes and designs required for the delivery of products and services. More important, is having an emotional connection and knowledge of the well-being of your team members within the framework of your organization and its purpose.

Step 5
The Creative Rebel

"If you are always trying to be normal, you will never know how amazing you can be."
- Maya Angelou

It takes courage to look outside the box and do something out of the ordinary or break the regular routine. Courage begins with an inward decision, but having courage is not an absence of fear. Fear can spark a movement.

You need:

1. Creativity
2. Innovation
3. To create a movement

Courage is doing what you may be afraid to do but you look beyond it and do it anyway.
Courage builds you up to go through open doors that lead to opportunities, which is one of its most wonderful benefits.

Dr. Martin Luther King, Jr. said, "The ultimate measure of a man is not where he stands in moments of comfort and convenience, but where he stands at times of challenge and controversy."

The Creative Rebel at Work

You have the will to take calculated risks, experiment with new systems, policies, and ways of doing things that previously may have been met with great resistance.

- **Creativity:** You will be the anchor that coordinates solutions to a particular issue or problem. You must have a dare to fail attitude and combine it with conceptual ideas to bring solutions that make for a competitive advantage in situations and circumstances.
- **Innovation:** You can generate the process of transforming your ideas into reality with a new dimension of performance within an organization, or within your life on a personal level.
- **Create a movement:** You must continue to press forward toward your dreams. Moving forward creates opportunities for growth and change. Imagine being aboard a ship that has its anchor down in the water. The ship will not be able to move to the next destination until the anchor is raised and movement begins. Lift the anchor and create movement.

You have a creative rebel within. Step into your creative awareness and own it! Once you take that step, success can and will always be just on the other side of your comfort zone.

Step 6
Perception vs Truth

Did you know that factors in a resilient environment does not happen by accident? They are fostered by intentional decisions and actions.

For example, when you are a supportive member in a team, group, relationship, or in a marriage, your ideas and concepts are easily accepted. It is a wonderful environment because to be your authentic self and have a sense of belonging is powerful.

You contribute your authenticity, skills, ideas, and talents. Successes are attributed to the mutually agreed to safety and sanctity of your trusted partner relationship, which applies to all members.

When you show up with these factors, half the battle is already won. Success comes with these attributes of expression. Power equals power, connections equal connections, and trust equal trust. Your greatness attributes are on the right track:

1. Psychological safety
2. Meaning of work
3. Impact of work

Leadership Attributes

Productive individuals and/or team members have your back. You count on each other to do high quality work on time. The structure, roles, goals, and execution plans are concrete, clear, and concise.

- **Psychological Safety:** You can be your authentic self within your team. Scrutiny and criticism are non-existent.
- **Meaning of Work**: You are working on something that is personally important to your entire team.
- **Impact of Work:** You fundamentally know that the work you're doing matters, and positively impacts the well-being of others.

You set intentions to foster mindfulness, to create a pathway for positive emotions. This simple action reduces negative emotions and stress. It creates a positive environment that can build resilience in individuals. You can recognize the power you have within, and your own inner strength. Combined, these lead you to the rewards in your life. You are the attribution factor and gift to the world given by God.

According to John Maxwell, "The pessimist complains about the wind. The optimist expects it to change, however; the leader adjusts the sails."

Step 7
Mind Your Courage

"Everything starts in your thoughts and words. Everything you think and believe about yourself or a situation determines what happens in your life. So, if you want to change your life, you need to stretch your mind."

-Wayne Dyer

Small shifts in your mindset can trigger a cascade of changes.

In this step, you will learn how to change the way you think.

1. Know who you are.
2. Your thoughts and mind control your body.
3. Have the courage to sink or swim.
   Be what you want. Do what you are.
   Have what you are.

Act on your faith so it can grow. Find the courage within yourself, in God, and in your higher consciousness authority. Take the mindset that you no longer accept things you cannot change, but you change the things you cannot accept. Imagine the possibility of change, and your new reality by changing your current situation.

Courage To Change

Did you know you need courage to change? You are what you think about, whether positive or negative. All it takes is twenty seconds of insane courage and all will change.

- **Know who you are.** You have the power within yourself to be courageous, strong, a fighter, a survivor, bold, assertive, fearful, proactive, or reactive. Do you know that a mindset embedded with insecurity is an inner-strength killer? You can be anything you set your mind to be.
- **Your thoughts and mind control your body.** Have faith, thoughts of confidence, and courage to stand up strongly for your rights and the liberty of others. Believe you can rise above challenges, fears, and stressful situations. Life-giving power resides in every spoken word. This leads to a win-win victory!
- **Have courage to sink or swim:** You have a choice to sink or swim in any challenge or scary situation. To sink is a metaphor for freezing and giving up all efforts. To swim is to actively do something to change the situation, the outcome, and the narrative for victory.

Step 8
Keep Calm in the Storm

A Bible scripture reads:

"Be strong and courageous. Do not be frightened and do not be dismayed." (Joshua 1:9)

This requires faith within yourself and connection to a higher source.

Faith is the substance of things you hope for and the beliefs that are yet invisible to the naked eye. Faith is the ability to see success before it happens. Faith thrives in uncertainty; it expands and rises to victory. In this step, you will learn the importance of faith.

1. Your safety depends on faith.
2. Faith leads to decisions and action.

Life is not about how to survive the storm, but how to dance in the rain.

Faith is the belief that you will prevail no matter what the situation or circumstance. You will rise despite the hostage and imprisonment feelings of fear. Do not be defeated by fears. Have faith and believe in your faith.

Faith: The Calm in the Storm

Life may not always be smooth sailing but keeping calm through the storm is often the best strategy. Keep calm and even laugh at life's craziness.

- **Your safety depends on faith.** Faith is contagious, a continual disposition despite the conditions, circumstances, or situations. Decisions are made through your faith. Your decisions are based on your internal belief system. They're manifested by what you desire and want. What do you believe? What are your intentions? What do you want?
- **Faith leads to action.** Having faith in yourself and a higher source is a powerful, untouchable, unstoppable force. Faith is assertive and sometimes aggressive. Faith is action. Without action, there is no faith; without faith, there is no action.
- **Faith, belief, and work.** Nothing will happen unless you work for it. Faith and work go hand in hand. Aside from that, you must believe and work to receive. For example, if you see a job that you want, the first thing to do is apply, then prepare for the interview, and last, believe you're qualified to have the job.

Step 9
Your Voice Holds Power

Did you know you can persevere and overcome anything by tapping into your inner strengths? In this step, we will discuss having the awareness of your strength to help prepare your safety.

You should be aware of:

1. Inner strength
2. Mental strength
3. Your inner source of power

The creative power of spoken words and conscious choice of words is like building with bricks and mortar. Words are the raw materials that form the lives we live. Words carry power. "Spoken words have power beyond measure"

-Debasiah Mridha

Did you know that you're a magnet attracting everything to you? The more you practice and realize that you are the greater magnet, you will become powerful in your faith, belief, and knowing.

"The best word shakers were the ones who understood the true power of words. They were the ones who climbed the highest."

-Mark Zusak

17

Your Voice Holds Power

"When everything seems to be going against you, remember that the airplane takes off against the wind, not with it." *- Henry Ford*

Imagine the following statement, "A closed mouth does not get fed." If we keep our mouths closed, we will never be able to feed ourselves.

- **Inner strength:** This is the strength of your soul, a wonderful soul. It is the core strength of your person. Your voice was made to be expressed and heard in positive ways.
- **Mental strength:** This is the strength of your mind. Your mind is for feeling, thinking, and solving problems. It is determined, firm, unyielding, and unshakeable.
- **You have an inner source of power:** Know who you are. Be intentional about what you believe about yourself. You have a natural instinct to survive. With this ability, your mind functions as the conduit or circuit of higher information conveyed to your higher self.

You can declare something and it will be established for you. The whole universe is waiting for you to give it instructions. Even though spoken words are not visible, they are substantive energy entities that bring tangibility to you from the universe through the power of God.

Step 10
The Real Value

Did you know you are the value? What you value and how you value yourself is how the world sees you. The secret to being the real value is the concept of love and wellness. To love yourself does not exclude loving others. The concept of wellness and self-care is akin to putting your own mask on before you help mask another.

Everyone's path is different, with varying obstacles, privileges, and purposes. Identifying diverse values in others and self can help navigate the unique path to enlightening the lives of others. Life becomes valued and honored. You are worthy and valuable.

Wellness values to live by:

1. Physical
2. Mental/Emotional
3. Spiritual
4. Social
5. Environmental

"Success is not final; failure is not fatal. It is the courage to continue that counts."

- Winston Churchill

Value: Well-Being, Happiness, Alignment

Imagine getting knocked down lower than you have ever been, but you stand back up taller than you ever were. There is value in getting back up and reflecting on the lesson in the knockdown.

When your well-being and happiness is in alignment with your values, the path is clear, and you will be unstoppable. Awaken the synergies and opportunities for forward movement and growth.

- **Physical:** Maintain a healthy body through exercise, nutrition, and sleep.
- **Mental:** Engage with the world through learning, problem-solving, and creativity.
- **Emotional:** Being in touch with, aware of accepting of, and able to express feelings (and those of others).
- **Spiritual:** Your search for meaning and purpose in human existence.
- **Social:** Connecting, interacting, and contributing with other people.
- **Environmental:** A healthy physical environment free of hazards, and your role to help make it better.

"Surround yourself with people who are going to lift you higher."

– Oprah Winfrey

Step 11
Self-Awareness

Did you know there's a name for those false inner beliefs telling you you're not worthy? Imposter syndrome. It's a false belief system connected to the lack of a confident mindset, victim mentality, and fear energy.

The feelings you have of insecurity, inadequacy, and incompleteness all stem from the same place: not knowing who you are within Christ—the higher source, or the connection you have in Him.

1. Carry yourself with authority.
2. Fear energy is rocket fuel.
3. Intuition is creative genius.

Your higher self is the profound version of oneself. The key is to transform your higher self every day. You can approach life reactively or proactively. Reactivity is your response to something that happens or occurs that forces you to respond.

A proactive approach is a way in which you progress forward in your life so that if anything happens out of the ordinary, you already know how to respond.

Growing Self-Awareness

"Be strong. Take courage. Do not be intimidated. Do not give them a second thought because God, your God, is striding ahead of you. He is right there with you. He won't let you down; he won't leave you." (Deuteronomy 31:6)

You have the knowledge within you.

- **Carry yourself with authority**: Stand tall with an aura of confidence. Look the part; make and maintain eye contact with people. Talk in a steady voice. You are as powerful as a superwoman or superman.
- **Fear energy is rocket fuel:** This is the turning point where you decide to manipulate your energy for good. It can take you places. Use this energy to your advantage and change the trajectory.
- **Intuition creative genius:** Your progressive forward movement; your best response to whatever shows up in your life that's out of the ordinary. You have the creative ability to make lemonade in any flavor.

Step 12
Transitions and Transformations

Transitions and transformations are two words that are related to each other. What thoughts come to your mind when you think of them? Do these words make you feel uncomfortable? Well, you are not alone.

One of the best ways to accept transitions and transformations is with the triple-A (AAA) framework for transformation.

1. Acknowledge
2. Accept
3. Action

You can look at the two words separately: transition is a gradual psychological and emotional process through which individuals and or groups reorient themselves so they can function and find meaning in a changed situation.

Transformation is a change of state, the passage from one way of being to another. You can modify your mindset, your core beliefs, and your behaviors in profound ways to achieve your desired results. Align yourself with intention, purpose, and expectancy.

Transitions and Transformations: IRONMAN Triathlon

When you think about life, it's a wonderful, blessed journey. You can view life in many ways. The IRONMAN triathlon is the epitome of athleticism, achieved through transitions, agility and adaptation in the face of challenges.

The IRONMAN triathlon uses three abstract symbols that represent a swimmer, a cyclist, and a runner. The symbols represent transitioning and transforming through life from one event to the next.

- **Acknowledge**: It is not your circumstances that matter, but your ability to tap into your higher source. The acknowledgment of your inner divine power allows you to complete the tasks ahead of you.
- **Accept:** You are uniquely made. Acceptance is crucial. Life brings things that will come, and things that will go. How you choose to respond is what matters. You are a gift from God.
- **Action:** You are bold as a lion. You can walk in truth, walk in faith, and walk in your power to succeed and overcome anything. Action will get you to the finish line with transformation and victory.

Step 13
Vessels for Victory

Do not look back; you are not going that way. Ask yourself, what your life would be like if you were stuck re-living the past? What type of impact would that have on your current situation?

Here's something to consider: the journey is much easier when you're not carrying your past in your current journey. Moving forward with belief in yourself can make a big difference in every area of your life.

Your life is composed of the creation of your emotions, mind, energy, and belief system. However, emotions are only a temporary state of being. This is true whether it's anger, sadness, or fear. Imagine the ability to manage your emotions in a way to change the way you think, to lead yourself to victorious outcomes.

Be the energy that you want to attract and see in your life. Be the energy of perseverance and victory. Here are the steps:

1. Intention
2. Prayer and faith
3. Instruction
4. Hope

Vessels of Prayer and Faith

You recognize that you may be in an altered status but you allow yourself to be vulnerable yet open for victory. You will be unstoppable, grow, and get the victory. "There is no such thing as failure. Failure is just life trying to move you in another direction."   *-Oprah Winfrey*

- **Intention:** What have you spoken or put in the atmosphere? The power of your spoken words make a difference. Those same words will come back to you in abundance. Your intentions have power, presence, and prophetic implications; they create a magnetic force.
- **Prayer and faith:** Build your faith through belief and prayer. Faith is like a muscle; it must be exercised. Faith can be weak or strong based on how much you use it. Use faith and prayer daily.
- **Instruction:** We must understand who we are as children of God and be receptive to the authority we have in Christ. Create order in every area of your life and move into a strategic plan with action.
- **Hope:** These are the things you think and hope for, the belief of things not seen. Get yourself instructed. Success is the fulfillment of divine purpose, while prosperity is having divine provisions to overcome obstacles.

Step 14
Modeling Love

Love doesn't cost anything. It is free and
unconditional to have and to give. What is love?
To love is a conscious decision for each
individual person. Love starts within, self-love. It
is what you become within first. Love is a choice.
Love is an action word, which means that you
show love by your actions.

One way to show love is in the ability to forgive.
Love and forgiveness are more than feelings;
they're an act of love accompanied by forgiveness. Giving love sets you free to forgive.

1. Forgive freely
2. Forge forward
3. Cancel the debt
4. Do not stop the flow

Forgive continually and completely. Stay in
peace and not in pieces. Forgiveness is for your
own good. Forgiveness helps you to propel and
keep moving forward in love. Real love is selfless
and free from fear.

When you send out real love, it returns to you.
Love is God in manifestation. Nothing is
 impossible where God operates!

Modeling Love for Forward Movement

A new commandment I give unto you, that you love one another. Love changes things in the world and the people of this world. Follow the path of love, and all things are added to your life and situations. (John 13:34)

Do to others as you would have them do to you. (Luke 6:3)

Whatever you do, do it with love. There is no agenda in love. Love is free.

- **Forgive freely.** Be good enough to forgive freely. You can't change other people's behavior. But you can change the way you view the behavior. This gives you the ability to soar to better things in life.
- **Forge forward.** Be free as a moving river of water. Move with intention and purpose through the debris along the river's path to gain the other side with love.
- **Cancel the debt.** Pure love doesn't punish or hold a grudge. Don't center your identity around a trauma you've experienced. Set yourself free to heal.
- **Don't stop the flow.** You can't reach for anything new if your hands are still full of yesterday's junk. Let go of the junk and let God's love step in. Let go in love and let God.

Step 15
Be the Light

What lies behind us and what lies before us are tiny matters compared to what lies within us.
- Ralph Waldo Emerson

You are what you think about. So, it would be in your best interest to fill your mind with good, godly, and great thoughts. Therefore, your light will shine. Light always illuminates the pathway in darkness.

Light unveils the heaviness in your heart and leads to all truth and a pathway for healing. Worries, heaviness, and a toxic environment can paralyze and weigh you down. But you have a choice. Choose to be the light.

1. See the light
2. Light illuminates
3. Be the light
4. Energy flows in the light

The sun rises and darkness resides every 12-plus hours. A new day arrives for a new beginning, purpose, and completion. Imagine your life without fear. Fear keeps you in darkness. Light sets you free!

Let Light Illuminate and Energy Flow

Sometimes when concepts are difficult for you to grasp or comprehend, you simply need to say, "Let there be light," the first recorded words God spoke. These four simple words can open your spirit and help you. Speak in faith. Speak these words over perplexing situations and watch God work.

- **See the light:** When you are wandering in the dark and you can't figure out what to do, seeing the light lets you obtain insight and wisdom.
- **Light illuminates:** You want your spirit and your mind to be illuminated to make the right choices and decisions. Light will reveal what you have been looking for right before your eyes.
- **Be the light:** Constant exposure to the light allows it to turn on and shine in you and through you.
- **Energy flows in the light:** This occurs when you stop focusing on the problem and start focusing on the answer—God's light. The solution will no longer be invisible to your sight and understanding.

You've finished. Before you go...

Tweet/Post/Share that you finished this book.

Please star rate this book.

Reviews are solid gold to writers. Please take a few minutes to give us some itty bitty feedback.

ABOUT THE AUTHOR

Natalie J. Clayton, MS, ACC is committed to share lessons authentically from life's journey through her intuitive abilities, guiding and leading you to overcome the transitions and transformations of life. She is the founder of the Coaching Group, TILT Synergy, Inc.

Natalie is a cancer survivor and "thriver" who is passionate about guiding and moving you through life's journey or challenges with faith, hope, light, and love. She believes whatever words or thoughts you give power to will have power over you. You are the leader within. You are the light. Shine your light.

Natalie helps people with her unique skill set as a Personal Development Coach. She enjoys empowering others through her coaching program, which provides tools to help you move toward transformation for a greater you.

www.nataliejclayton.com

If you enjoyed this Itty Bitty® Book you may also like…

- **Your Amazing Itty Bitty® Be The Boss Now Book -** Gregory Cendana

- **Your Amazing Itty Bitty® Productivity Book -** Matt Malouf

- **Your Amazing Itty Bitty® What Happen When Book** - Sharón Lynn Wyeth

Or any of the other Amazing Itty Bitty® Books available online at www.ittybittypublishing.com